Degas
and the Little Dancer

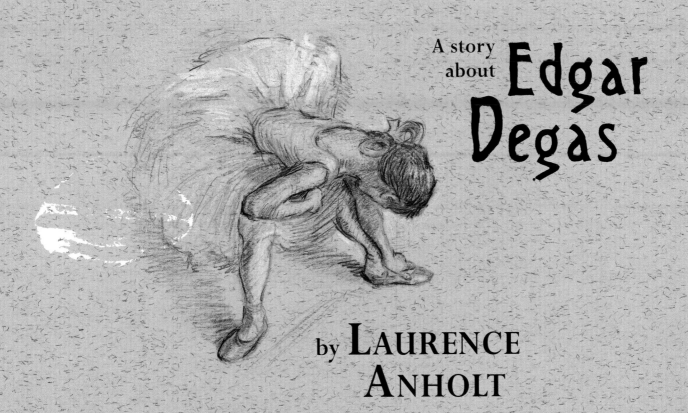

A story about **Edgar Degas**

by **LAURENCE ANHOLT**

BARRON'S

In the middle of a big room, in a famous art museum,
is a beautiful sculpture of a little dancer. She stands with
one foot forward, her hands clasped behind her back.
She looks tired and a bit sad.

The sculpture was made more than a hundred years ago
by an artist called Edgar Degas.

The guard who looks after the room in the museum
has a story to tell about the little ballerina. When it
is raining outside and people have nowhere else to go,
someone is sure to ask who she was.

"Her name is Marie," says the guard. "I look
at her standing there everyday, and I think I know
her pretty well..."

. . . Marie and her parents were very poor, but Marie dreamed of only one thing—she wanted to be a dancer. Not just any dancer: she wanted to dance at the Paris Opera House. She wanted to be the most famous ballerina in the world.

Marie's father was a tailor and her mother took in laundry. They worked hard and saved their money, until the day Marie was ready to take the entrance exam for the big ballet school.

Her father made her a special tutu, and her mother wished her luck, and tied a long peach-colored ribbon in her hair.

At the exam, Marie danced as she had never danced
before, and the old ballet teacher seemed to like her.

"If we give you a place," he said, "you will have
to practice very hard."

"I know," said Marie, "I want to be the most
famous dancer in the world."

Everyone laughed. "We'll see about that!" said
the old teacher.

It was the most exciting day of Marie's life. She couldn't wait to tell her family all about it; but just as she was about to rush home, something happened that almost spoiled her happiness.

At the back of the big room, someone started shouting. A girl ran past Marie in tears. She was followed by a fierce, gray-bearded man, dressed in expensive clothes.

"Why can't you keep still?" he shouted. "How can I draw you when you keep moving?"

Marie was frightened.

"Who is that bad-tempered man?" she whispered to the girl beside her.

"You will soon find out if you are a pupil here. That is Degas, painter of horses and dancers, and he treats them all the same."

At the museum, a large crowd has gathered around
the statue of the little ballerina.

   "Look at her," says the guard. "Look at little Marie.
I'll tell you something—if you stare at her long enough,
she almost seems to move!"

   "So, did she get her place at the ballet school?"
someone asks.

"Oh, yes," says the guard, "she got her place all right.
She worked hard, practicing her pirouettes and whatnot.
In fact, she became so good that the old teacher began to
talk about giving her the star part in the Christmas Ballet
at the Opera House..."

. . . Marie's dream was coming true.

And even old Degas didn't seem quite so frightening.
Everyday he turned up with his top hat and his sketch books,
muttering and cursing everyone. He worked furiously with
colored chalks, sketching the girls, the teachers, and
the musicians.

"Keep still!" he would shout. "Not like that. Like this . . . !"
Then he would show some poor dancer how to hold a pose
or to skip properly.

Marie had to try hard not to laugh at the sight of the
smartly dressed painter balancing on one leg.

Sometimes, Marie caught a glimpse of his sketches,
and what she saw made her gasp—the drawings almost
glowed with color. There were studies of all the girls,
but they didn't look like ballet stars.

Degas had drawn them...

chattering,

stretching,

tying their laces,

adjusting their straps—

even reading
a newspaper.

Marie loved her dancing. She was the first to arrive in the morning and the last to go home at night.

Then, one day, everything started to go wrong.

Marie's father became ill, and soon he couldn't work anymore. Her mother took in extra washing, but there simply wasn't enough money to pay for all Marie's classes.

Her dream of becoming a famous dancer began to fade.

"I would love to help you, Marie," said the kind old teacher, "but unless you have lessons everyday I will have to give the main part to someone else. Perhaps we could find a little work for you, sweeping the floor in the theater or..."

A gruff voice interrupted them.

"I will give you a few francs if you pose for me, but you will have to work very hard and not chatter. Do you understand?"

So Degas began to draw Marie every afternoon. He made her stand absolutely still for such a long time that Marie almost cried, but she didn't dare to complain.

The money was not enough. It paid for a doctor for her father, but not for the classes Marie needed. As the Christmas Ballet drew near, she knew she would never have the chance to become famous.

When the big night came, poor Marie was not even allowed to watch, because Degas wanted to work late.

While the other girls laughed and chattered and made themselves ready, Marie was left alone with the artist. More irritable than ever, he made her stand, looking up at the ceiling, with her hands behind her back. All the dancers were used to this pose, but as Degas worked on and on, Marie's neck began to ache.

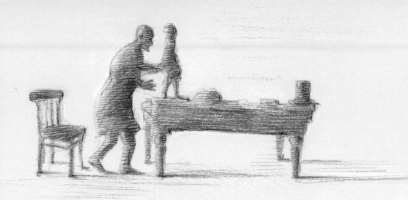

It was getting late.

"Excuse me, Monsieur Degas," Marie whispered.
"I will have to go home soon. My father is ill and my
family will be worried."

"Family!" shouted Degas. "Your family will be
worried? Do you know who will worry about me?
No one, that's who. I have only my work for company
and now even my eyesight is leaving me."

"I'm sorry, Monsieur, I don't understand."

Degas worked in silence for a while. He pulled
out some clay and began to work furiously with his
long fingers. Then Marie saw a tear in the artist's eye.

"No," he said more gently, "how could you understand?
Tell me, Marie, what is the most precious thing to a painter?"

"Your eyes, Monsieur?"

"Exactly. My eyes! Just like a dancer's legs, you understand? And *my* poor eyes are sick, Marie. That is why I am working with clay, because I can hardly see what I am doing anymore."

Suddenly Marie felt very sad for the bad-tempered artist. Could this be why he was always angry?

"I am very sorry," she said.

Then Degas did something Marie had never seen him do before. He looked up at her and smiled.

"I am sorry, too, Marie," he said. "But look at the sculpture. It's the best thing I've ever done. Thank you, my little dancer. Now you must go home."

Marie stepped down. Her legs were weak. She untied the peach-colored ribbon from her hair and gave it to the old artist. Then she put away her dancing clothes and ran home to her family.

In the theater, the crowds clapped and cheered
as the curtain came down on the Christmas Ballet.
Outside, under a pale streetlight, an old, nearly blind
artist struggled home alone.

In his hand he clutched a peach-colored ribbon.

"*And so she never did find her dream?*" someone asks.
"*Wait,*" says the guard. "*The story isn't quite finished…*"

Two years later Marie was helping her mother with
the laundry when a letter arrived at 36, Rue de Douai.

"It's for you, Marie," said her mother.

Marie tore open the envelope. Inside was a ticket
and an invitation to a big art exhibition. On the invitation
someone had scribbled "For Marie, the little dancer."

Marie and her mother went to the show. The building
was very crowded. The walls were hung with brilliantly
colored paintings, but the biggest crowd was gathered
around a large glass box.

Marie pushed through the crowd.

"Look!" she gasped. "It's me!"

Degas had dressed the sculpture in real clothes.
No one had seen anything like it before. In her hair
was the peach-colored ribbon.

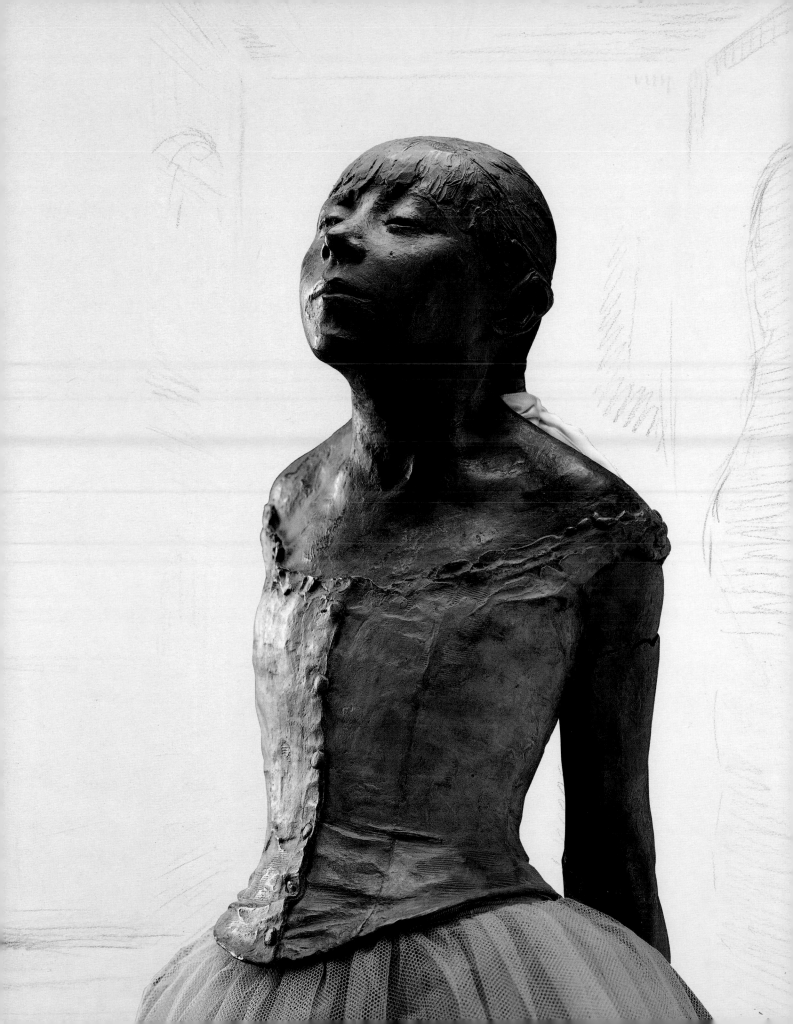

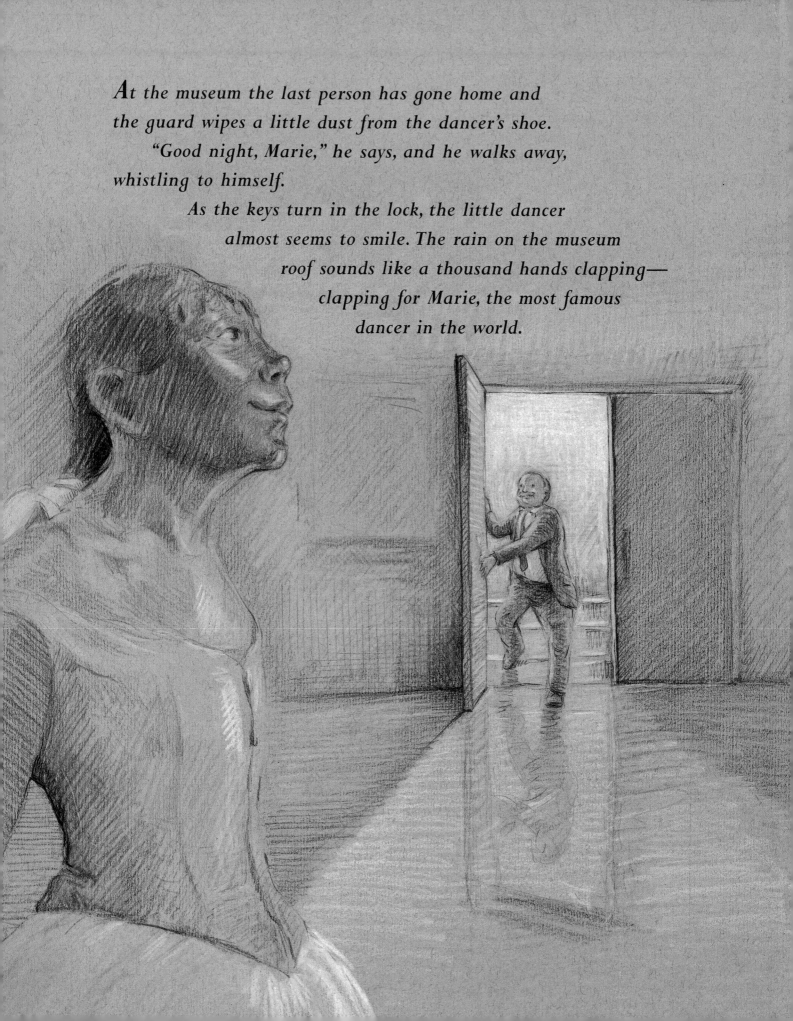

At the museum the last person has gone home and
the guard wipes a little dust from the dancer's shoe.
"Good night, Marie," he says, and he walks away,
whistling to himself.
As the keys turn in the lock, the little dancer
almost seems to smile. The rain on the museum
roof sounds like a thousand hands clapping—
clapping for Marie, the most famous
dancer in the world.